P9-DDM-137

BARD OF AVON
The Story of
William Shakespeare

DIANE STANLEY AND PETER VENNEMA
ILLUSTRATED BY DIANE STANLEY

MORROW JUNIOR BOOKS
New York

To Catherine,
my firstborn,
my thespian
D.S.

The authors would like to thank Dr. William B. Hunter,
who inspired this book and whose help was invaluable in writing it.

The full-color artwork was done in gouache, opaque watercolor paint,
on Fabriano watercolor paper. The text type is 14 point Bernhard Modern.

Text copyright © 1992 by Diane Stanley and Peter Vennema
Illustrations copyright © 1992 by Diane Stanley

Printed in Singapore at Tien Wah Press.
1 2 3 4 5 6 7 8 9 10
Library of Congress Cataloging-in-Publication Data
Stanley, Diane.
Bard of Avon : the story of William Shakespeare / by Diane Stanley
and Peter Vennema ; illustrated by Diane Stanley.
p.   cm.
Includes bibliographical references.
Summary: A brief biography of the world's most famous playwright,
using only historically correct information.
ISBN 0-688-09108-3 (trade)—ISBN 0-688-09109-1 (library)
1. Shakespeare, William, 1564–1616—Biography—Juvenile
literature.   2. Dramatists, English—Early modern, 1500–1700—
Biography—Juvenile literature.   [1. Shakespeare, William,
1564–1616.   2. Dramatists, English.   3. Poets, English.]
I. Vennema, Peter.   II. Title.
PR2895.S7   1992
822.3'3—dc20   [92]   [B]
90-46564   CIP   AC

Authors' Note

William Shakespeare is one of the most famous men who ever lived. Yet much of his life is a mystery to us. He did not keep a diary, and none of his personal letters has survived. We do not even know exactly when he was born—only the date on which his baptism was registered. We know a little about his parents, his wife, and his children. Besides his plays and poems, the only other documents we have are business transactions, court papers, and his will.

Of course, we know a great deal about the times in which he lived—of Queen Elizabeth and King James, and the great men who admired and encouraged Shakespeare's work. His friends and fellow writers have left us bits of information in their books and letters. After he died, many tales about his life were told, though we do not know which—if any of them—are true.

In writing this story, we have tried to show how historians investigate a life lived long ago. Like detectives, historians gather all the known facts together until a pattern begins to appear. And when that pattern reveals the life of one of the most exceptional writers of all time, what an exciting discovery that is!

In the year 1569, a company of traveling actors came to the little English town of Stratford-on-Avon. As their cart rolled into the town square, the high bailiff, or mayor, greeted the actors and led them to the guildhall where they would do a special performance for him. If he liked the play, he would give them a license to present it to the public.

The high bailiff was John Shakespeare, a prosperous glove maker. He was pleased and agreed to pay the Queen's Players nine shillings—less than fifty dollars today. Perhaps he allowed his five-year-old son, William, to sit in front with him for the special performance. If so, it was the first play he ever saw.

The actors were given permission to perform, so they began to unload their cart. They set out trestles in the courtyard of an inn and laid long boards over them for a stage. They hung a curtain behind it as a backdrop and took out their costumes and props. Soon they were ready to entertain the good folk of Stratford.

We don't know what play they performed. Perhaps they did *Ralph Roister Doister*, a funny play with characters named Matthew Merrygreek and Margery Mumblecrust. Or it may have been a tragedy about some great hero, with lots of sword fighting and dramatic speeches. Doubtless, the people loved it and talked about it long afterward, for public entertainment was rare in those days. From then on, traveling players came to Stratford almost every year, and it was always a special event.

When William was six or seven, he entered the local grammar school. It was a good school for its day, and it was free, though only boys could go. The schoolmaster taught the younger boys to read and write. In another part of the room, he led the older boys in the study of Latin and Greek. They memorized long passages of poetry in those languages. William had an amazing memory, and years later he frequently referred to the myths and history of his childhood study in the great plays he wrote.

William graduated from Stratford Grammar School when he was sixteen. By then, the Shakespeare family had fallen on hard times. John Shakespeare owed money. He could not pay his taxes. He was no longer a town leader and, at one point, didn't even go to church for fear of being arrested for debt. Obviously, there was no money for a university education.

So William Shakespeare went to work, but we don't know what he did. He probably helped his father make gloves, though some people think that he was a schoolmaster's assistant and others that he worked for a lawyer.

Only one thing is certain: when William Shakespeare was eighteen years old, he got married to Anne Hathaway, who was twenty-six. John and Mary Shakespeare were probably against the marriage. First of all, the family was short of money. And the house on Henley Street must have been crowded and noisy enough already, for William had three brothers and two sisters, and the youngest of them was only three. Even so, William brought his new wife to live with them, and when their daughter Susanna was born, six months later, there were ten people in the house. Less than two years later, there were twelve, when Anne gave birth to twins, Hamnet and Judith.

Some time after that, William left Stratford and went to London. No one knows when he left or under what circumstances.

Anne, Susanna, and the twins stayed behind in Stratford. We assume that Will sent money to support them, and came sometimes to visit. But he never took them to London to live with him, and he and Anne had no more children. It does not appear that they had a very happy marriage.

William Shakespeare went to London just at the time when modern theater was taking shape. In 1576, when Shakespeare was still a schoolboy, an actor named James Burbage put up a building near London designed solely for the performance of plays. It was the first such building since the days of ancient Greece and Rome. He called it the Theatre, a name now used for all playhouses.

The people of London loved to see plays, and James Burbage's Theatre was a smash success. Soon other playhouses were built, first the Curtain, then the Rose and the Swan.

These new theaters were circular wooden buildings with an open courtyard in the middle, much like the inn yards in which plays were often performed. People could stand in the courtyard for a penny. They were called groundlings, and they were known to drink too much beer and be quite noisy and rude if they didn't like the play. A wise playwright would throw in a joke every now and then to keep the groundlings happy.

Anyone willing to pay a bit more could sit in one of the three galleries, where they had a roof to protect them from the sun or a sudden shower.

Plays were only done in daylight and in nice weather, as there were no lights or heat. On the days when a play would be presented, a flag was flown from the tower of the theater, where people in the city could see it.

There was no curtain across the stage and not much scenery. A table and chairs would show that it was a banquet room; a potted bush would represent the countryside. Sometimes a sign was carried onstage telling the location, such as A WOOD NEAR ATHENS. Or an actor would walk onstage and say something such as, "Well, this is the Forest of Arden!"

The costumes were often elegant. In those days, it was customary for a gentleman to leave his clothes to his faithful servants when he died. But servants didn't wear that sort of clothing, so they sold it to the actors to wear as costumes.

A WOOD NEAR ATHENS

A Midsummer Night's Dream

The theaters also had special effects. The roof of the stage, painted with stars and called the heavens, had a trapdoor in it. If the play called for a god to descend from the sky, a throne could be lowered through the trapdoor by ropes. The sound of thunder was made by rolling a cannonball around on the floor of the hut above the stage. There was also a cannon up there that fired blanks for the battle scenes.

Just as there was a "heavens," there was also a "hell." This was the area under the stage, and it had a trapdoor, too, through which actors could appear or disappear as the play might require.

In Elizabethan plays, the death scenes were very realistic. The actor to be "stabbed" would hide a pouch of pig's blood under his shirt. This would burst when his opponent stabbed him, much to the delight of the groundlings.

Heavens

Hell

It is fortunate that Queen Elizabeth and her friends at court loved plays, for there was a powerful religious group, known as the Puritans, who wanted to close the theaters. The Puritans were very strict in their morals, and they thought plays were "sinful, heathenish, lewd, and ungodly." They also believed the theater attracted unruly crowds and criminals, which, in fact, it did.

The Puritans might have put an end to this new art if the queen and her courtiers had not given the actors their protection. A nobleman would adopt a company of actors and allow them to make use of his name, such as the Admiral's Men or Lord Chamberlain's Men. At one time, even Elizabeth had her own actors, the Queen's Men. In return, the actors would give special performances for their patron, either in the great halls of their estates or at the palace. The prestige of their patron's name went with them, even when acting in one of the new theaters or touring in the countryside.

In spite of all the influential help, the Puritans still managed to drive the players outside the London city limits, where all the famous Elizabethan theaters were built.

Each acting company had about twelve men, who often stayed together for years. There would always be a leading man and a comedian, as well as someone (like Shakespeare) who played "kingly" and older men's parts. There were also character actors and boy apprentices.

Shakespeare had to keep in mind the actors who would perform his play: whether they were young or old, thin or fat, and what sort of parts they played best.

All the players were men, as it was not considered proper for women to be actors. Women's parts were played by boys who were young enough to have a high voice and, of course, no beard.

The company would hire extra actors for small parts and crowd scenes. Since the plays often called for music, musicians were also hired.

The new theaters couldn't keep on doing the same stale farces and melodramas that had charmed country audiences. They needed fresh material, something more sophisticated for city people who went to the theater regularly.

Soon a group of brilliant and educated young men began putting their talents to writing plays. These University Wits, as they were called, wrote complicated and beautiful stories with magnificent poetry and lots of action. The greatest of these young playwrights was Christopher Marlowe.

When we pick up Shakespeare's trail again, in 1592, we find that he is working in London as an actor and has written a play, *Henry VI*. It must have been a popular play, for one of the Wits was so jealous, he described Shakespeare in a pamphlet as "an upstart crow, beautified with our feathers." He was insulted that a common actor would presume to write plays.

Despite the wits, Shakespeare had gotten his start as an actor and a playwright. But soon, an outbreak of the plague hit London, and all the theaters were closed for two years. The authorities believed that large gatherings of people would spread the disease.

Shakespeare took this time to write two long poems, *Venus and Adonis* and *The Rape of Lucrece*. He dedicated them to the Earl of Southampton, who paid him handsomely for the honor. Shakespeare was very grateful to Southampton for paying him so well. From that time on, he would never be poor again. And he would remain loyal to the young earl in the difficult times ahead.

It may have been during these early years that Shakespeare wrote his series of short poems, or sonnets—though they were published much later. Some of the poems were written to a "fair youth" and others to a "dark lady." There was also a "rival poet." Historians have been trying ever since to discover who these important people in Shakespeare's life might have been.